In the Beginning God
Created the Earth...

the Land

The Bible Tells Me So Press

In the Beginning God Created the Earth...
the Land

A children's book produced by
The Bible Tells Me So Press

PUBLISHED BY
THE BIBLE TELLS ME SO CORPORATION
WWW.THEBIBLETELLSMESO.COM

First Printing, November 2021

God purposefully
and skillfully
created the earth
in many wonderful
ways.

One of the most
amazing things
about the earth
is...

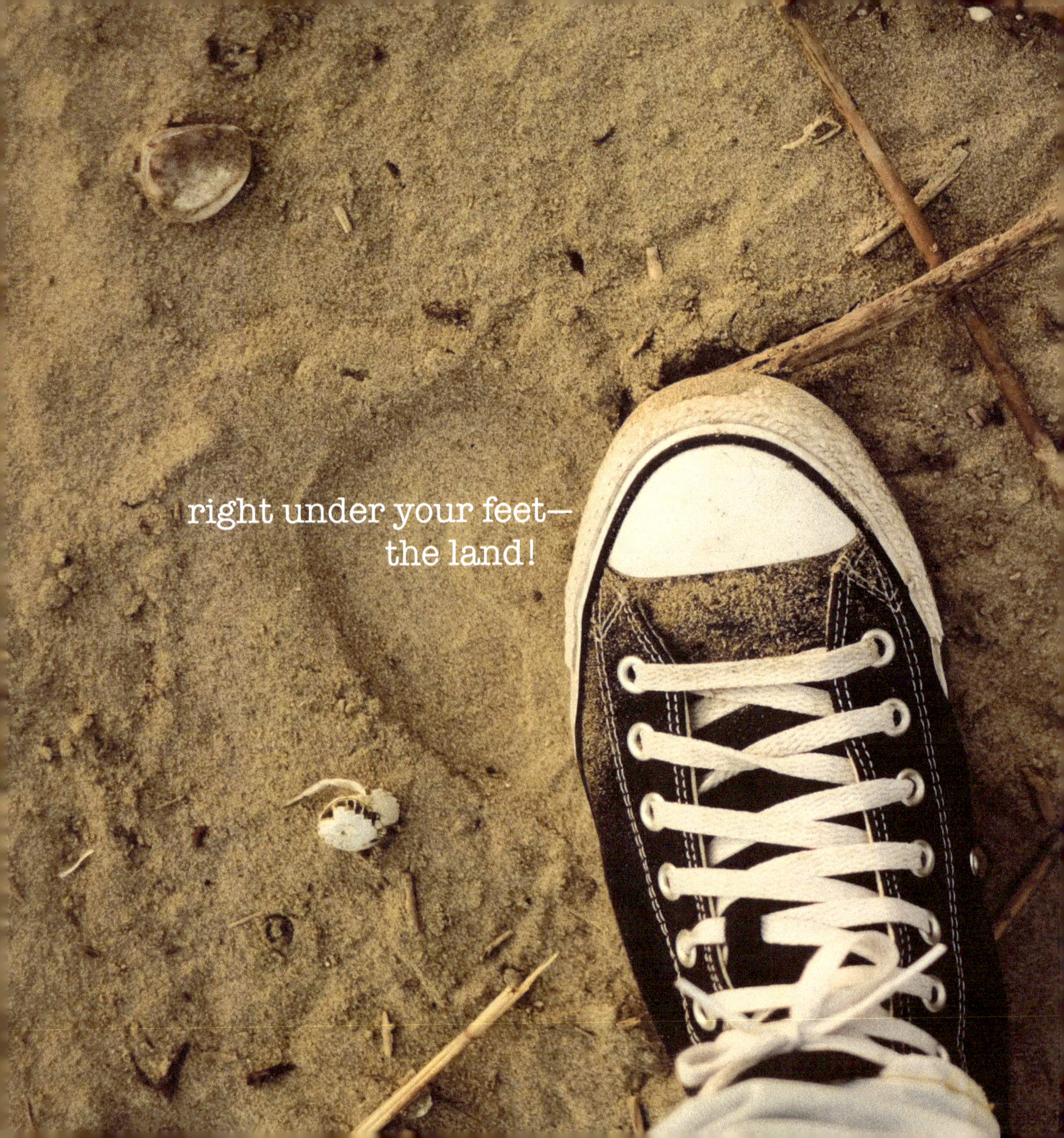

right under your feet—
the land!

When God created the land,
He wisely made it to be able to
move—to shift,
rise, and fall—
so that He could
design mountains,

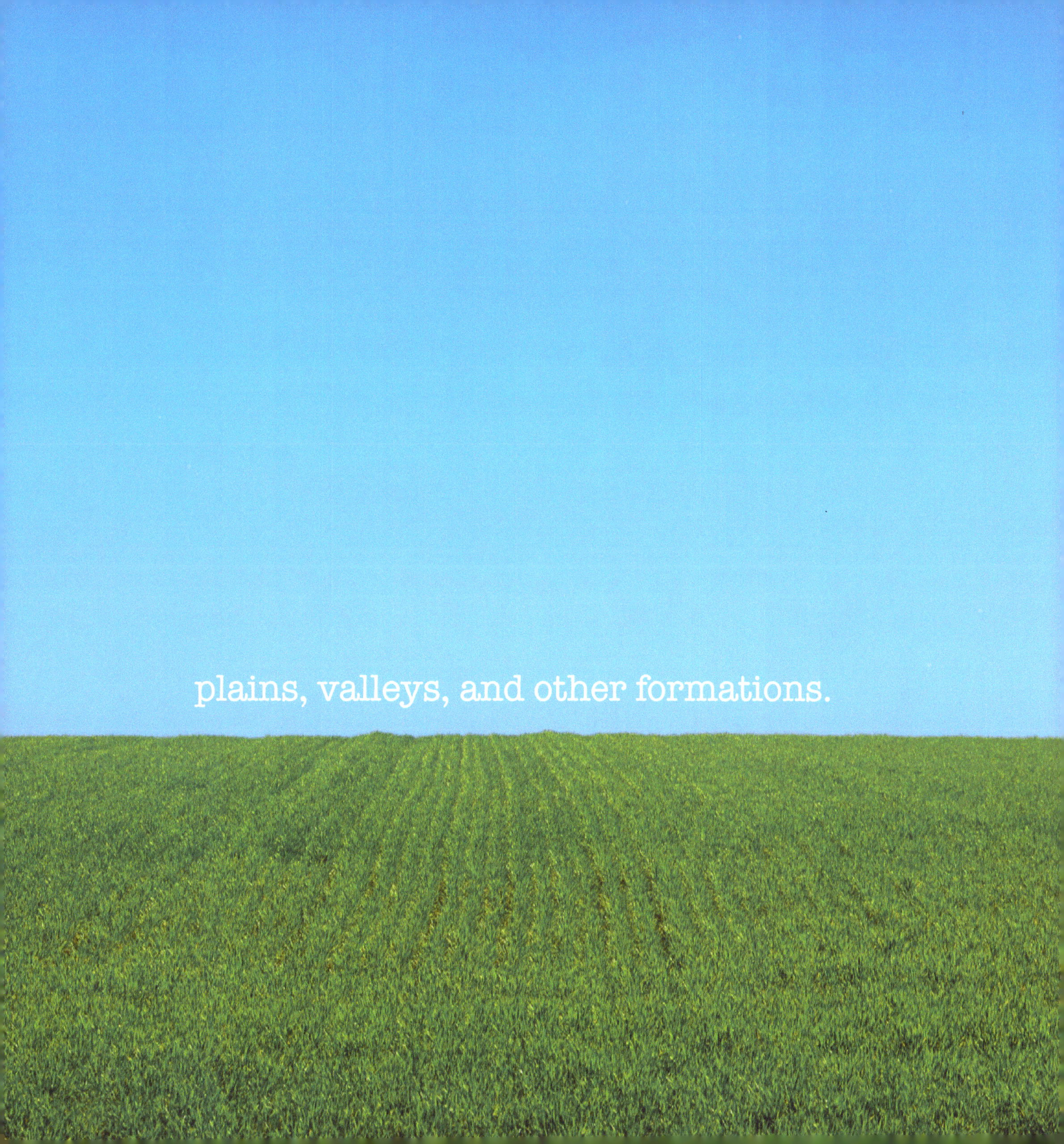

plains, valleys, and other formations.

Mountains are big and tall.

They are also very useful.

The cold temperatures on the tops of mountains are perfect for frozen water to fall from the clouds as snow.

Mountains are
a big part of an amazing
water-delivery
system.

When snow melts,
the water flows down
mountains as rivers
and streams

until it reaches us!

God also wisely
designed the earth to have flatlands.

Prairies and grasslands
are full of plants and animals.

Big animals, like elephants,

enjoy eating the food that grows there.

Even small animals, like this cute little prairie dog, love to live in these wide-open spaces.

Large flatlands are also perfect
for people to build farms and ranches
to grow crops and raise animals

or to build
big cities
where thousands,
even millions,
of people
can live.

But that's not all.
Plants, animals, and people
live in deep and beautiful
canyons and valleys too.

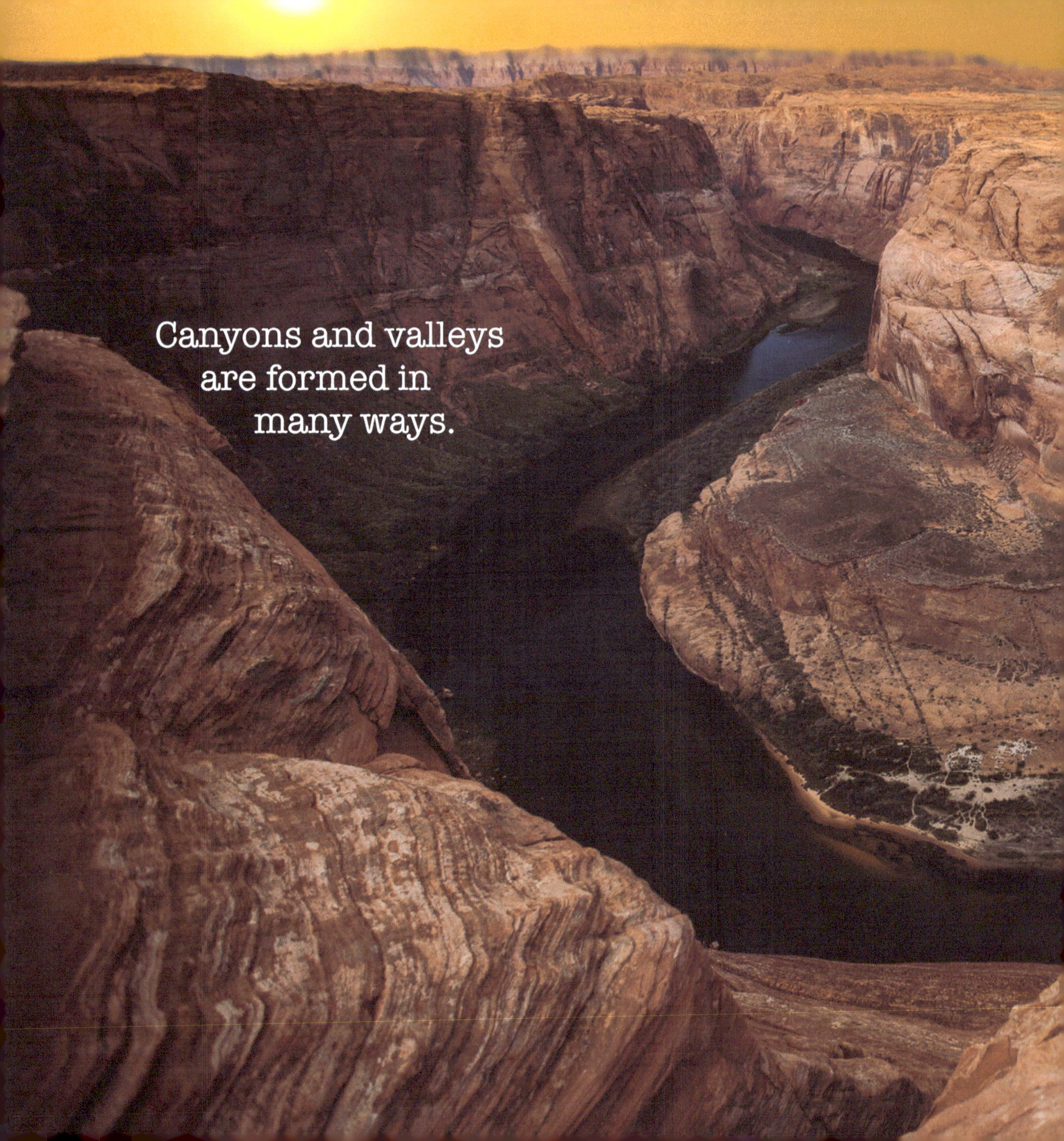

Canyons and valleys are formed in many ways.

Some are carved
out of the land
by water or ice.

God wisely created
and carefully designed
all of the earth's land

to be
just what
we need.

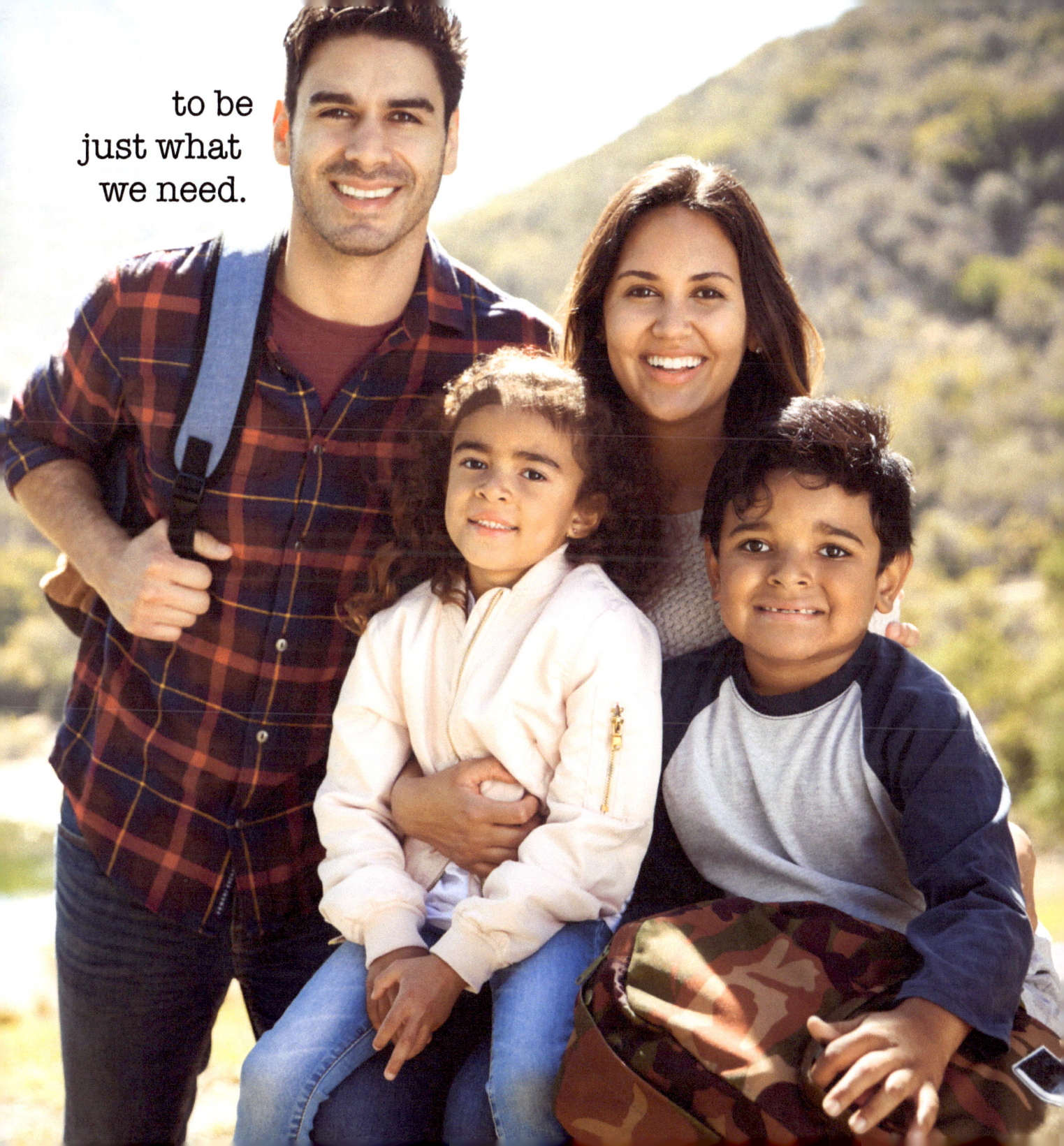

It was no accident,
and it didn't
happen
by chance.

Earth's land
is perfect for us
because God
made it that way.

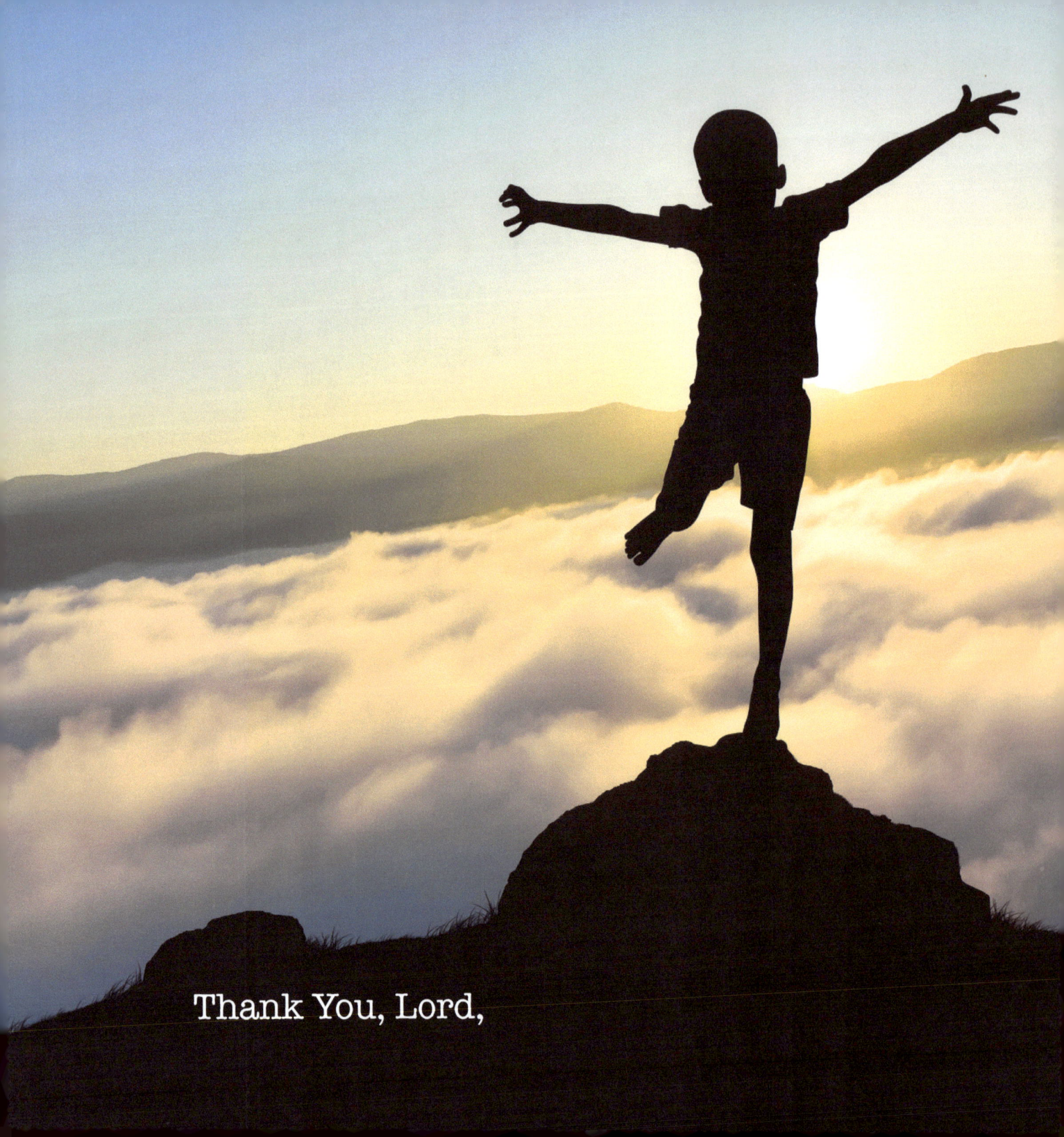

Thank You, Lord,

for
the beautiful,
useful, and
amazing land!

Indeed,
My hand laid
the foundations
of the earth.

Isaiah 48:13a

For more
books, videos, songs, and crafts,
visit us online at
TheBibleTellsMeSo.com

Standing on the Bible and growing!

www.ingramcontent.com/pod-product-compliance
Lightning Source LLC
Chambersburg PA
CBHW042103040426
42448CB00002B/120